The Sphynx:
The Hairless Cat

Jennifer Quasha

The Rosen Publishing Group's
PowerKids Press™
New York

Published in 2000 by The Rosen Publishing Group, Inc.
29 East 21st Street, New York, NY 10010

First Edition

Book Design: Michael de Guzman

Photo Credits: pp. 1, 16 © Reuters/Corbis-Bettmann; pp. 4, 8, 11, 19, 20, 22 © Henry Ausloos/Animals Animals; p. 7 © Tetsu Yamazaki/International Stock; p. 12 © UPI/Corbis-Bettmann; p. 15 © Robert Pearcy/Animals Animals.

Quasha, Jennifer.
    The Sphynx: the hairless cat / by Jennifer Quasha.
        p.   cm. — (A kid's cat library)
    Includes index.
    Summary: Discusses the origin, history, and characteristics of the hairless cat known as the Sphynx.
    ISBN 0-8239-5511-7
    1. Sphynx cat—Juvenile literature. [1. Sphynx cat. 2. Cats.]   I. Title. II. Series: Quasha, Jennifer. Kid's cat library.
SF449.S68Q36   1999
636.8—dc21
                                                                                          98-53563
                                                                                             CIP
                                                                                              AC

Manufactured in the United States of America

Contents

The Sphynx

The Sphynx is a very strange-looking cat that has no fur. It is the only hairless cat **breed**. Being hairless is not the only **characteristic** that makes the Sphynx different from other cats, though. The Sphynx has large ears, and its skin is loose and wrinkled. Another unusual characteristic of the Sphynx is its **stance**. Sphynxes are known to stand with one front paw lifted off the ground. Sphynx cats may look a little strange, but they are fun and playful animals.

◄ *Other animals besides the Sphynx, like dogs and mice, are sometimes hairless, but this is very rare.*

The Feel of the Hairless Cat

When the Sphynx is born it is covered with short, soft hairs. As it grows older these hairs fall out. If you've never petted a hairless cat before, it might feel strange. When you touch the Sphynx's skin it feels soft and fuzzy, like **suede**. Some people say it feels more like a peach. The Sphynx is warm to the touch. Its body temperature is four degrees higher than most cats. The warmth and feel of the Sphynx reminds people of a hot water bottle.
Because of this, the Sphynx has often been called a "suede hot water bottle."

The Sphynx's hairless skin might feel strange to touch at first. ▶

The Color of the Sphynx

Sphynx cats come in many different colors, just like cats with fur. If the Sphynx had fur, wherever the skin was pink, the fur would be white. Wherever the skin was dark, the Sphynx would have dark-colored fur. Some Sphynxes are all one dark color. These cats are called blues, because the dark color of their skin is bluish-gray. If a blue Sphynx had fur, it would probably be gray.

If this Sphynx had fur, the bluish-gray parts on its head and back would be gray, and the pinkish parts on its legs and body would be white.

Special Treatment

The Sphynx needs some special treatment because it is hairless. All cats' skin produces oils. You don't notice it on cats with fur because their fur **absorbs** the oil. Also, unlike cats with fur, the Sphynx sweats. The Sphynx has no fur to absorb sweat and oil, so it needs to be cleaned daily. Since the Sphynx has no fur to **protect** its skin, it needs to be guarded from cold weather and the sun. In winter, some Sphynx owners have their cat wear a sweater. If its skin isn't covered in the summer, the Sphynx can get sunburned.

Since they don't have fur, Sphynxes need to stay inside most of the time. ▶

Sphynx or Sphinx?

The name of the Sphynx came from the ancient Greek word, sphinx. The sphinx is a **mythical** animal that has the head of a human and the body of a lion. The sphinx is a part of many ancient Greek and Egyptian stories. In front of **tombs** in Egypt, you will sometimes see statues or pictures of sphinxes. The ancient Egyptians believed that cats had special powers. They thought that after someone died, cats and sphinxes would guard him in the afterlife.

◀ *The large statue is an Egyptian sphinx, built around the year 2500 B.C. to honor the dead King Khafre.*

Early History

The first hairless cats that we know of today were **bred** in the 1300s and 1400s by people called **Aztecs**. Many **artifacts** that look like Sphynx cats have been found from this time. In Mexico, where the Aztecs used to live, people have found paintings, statues, and carvings that look like this early hairless cat.

At the same time, the Aztecs also developed a hairless dog. Though the hairless dog still exists, the first breed of hairless cat does not. This type of hairless cat is now **extinct**.

A hairless cat that looked like today's Sphynx lived long ago in Mexico. ▶

14

United States
of America

Mexico

The First Sphynx

The first modern-day Sphynx was born in Toronto, Canada in 1966. This kitten was named Prune because of his wrinkly skin. Prune had no fur, but his parents did. Prune's mother was a longhaired cat. Surprisingly, many mothers and fathers of Sphynx cats have hair. Though more hairless cats were bred from Prune's mother, not enough were born for the breed to spread. This **lineage** of the Sphynx did not continue.

◀ *Sphynx cats often look worried because of the wrinkled skin on their foreheads.*

Hairless Cats in Canada

In 1978, another longhaired mother cat and her hairless kittens were rescued from the street in Toronto, Canada. One of the kittens was brought to a country called the Netherlands and bred to make more hairless cats. This was the first time that Sphynx cats were healthy and continued to have babies that looked just like them. Almost all Sphynx cats today are related to this family of rescued kittens.

The Sphynx is not totally hairless. Its tail, face, ears, and feet have a very light covering of fur. ▶

The Sphynx in Cat Shows

The first Sphynx to compete in a cat show was entered in 1971. It did not win any prizes. Later, a Sphynx called E.T. was shown at the Madison Square Garden Cat Show in the 1980s. Some people don't want Sphynx cats to be allowed in cat shows. This is because they believe that the Sphynx should not be bred anymore. They think that because it has no fur to protect it, it is not healthy.

◀ *Many people at the cat show thought that E.T. was ugly because he had no fur.*

The Pet Sphynx

Though the Sphynx may not be the fluffiest of cats, it is a sweet, friendly pet. Sphynx cats are known to enjoy being around people and other animals. Sphynxes are lively and are always ready to play and explore. Sphynx cats are loving pets that like to cuddle up with their owners. These unusual cats are fun to look at and a joy to own.

Web Sites:

http://www.sphynx.org/history.html
http://www.breedlist.com/sphynx-breeders.html

Glossary

absorb (ub-ZORB) To take something in and hold it there.

artifact (AR-tih-fakt) Any object made by people.

Aztecs (AZ-teks) An ancient group of people who lived in what is now Mexico.

bred (BRED) When people have brought a male and a female animal together so that they will have babies.

breed (BREED) A group of animals that look very much alike and have the same kind of relatives.

characteristic (KAR-ik-tuh-RIH-stik) A special mark or part of something.

extinct (ik-STINKT) To no longer exist.

lineage (LIH-nee-ij) Family history.

mythical (MIH-thih-cul) Imaginary.

protect (pruh-TEKT) To keep from harm.

stance (STANTS) The way an animal or person stands.

suede (SWAYD) A soft leather made from a calf's skin.

tomb (TOOM) A place where the dead are buried.

Index